D1550404

Best wishes,
John S. Brinkerhoff

DINOSAURS

Also by the Author:
All in Time

John Scott Brinkerhoff

DINOSAURS

THE GOLDEN QUILL PRESS
Publishers
Francestown   New Hampshire

Library of Congress Catalog Card Number 80-83885

ISBN 0-8233-0326-8

Printed in the United States of America

For G'Anne
as always, with love

ACKNOWLEDGMENTS

Several of the poems in this volume have appeared elsewhere. *kenilworth; marion, ohio; the real world;* and *Terra Nova, 1912* were published in *The Cornfield Review* through the encouragement of its creator Dr. David Citino of the Ohio State University Marion campus. *commuter* appeared in *Kaleidoscope Magazine*, published in South Carolina.

CONTENTS

Maybe We'll Live

brian at 9
(St. Augustine Beach)

his small, bony hands shape the sand
                              in windy light.
pressing. smoothing. a gift
for his eyes, and the mother sea.
                              my heart
carves the windows.

he leaves for the waves;
looks out to where the clouds come down.
I can see that he's puzzled,
bothered by some memory
that will not show itself.

he walks the soft edge,
                    listening,
as a seagull follows   like a well-dressed   friend.

9

FIRST LIGHT

antaeus perceives his mistress

I

We do not plunge into the dream, but glide
as mist about the paws of dogs,
curl upon ourselves in shuffling sleep, slide
between the object and the reflection,
think back to future road-winds, smell songs
of ribboned fields awheel with birds,
of pale child legs stretched in streams hung
with summer's bones
and discover the hand in its absence
the tongue in its silence
the eye in its gathering gloom . . . .

II

I'm told that the river,
in itself, is not. As without sense or source or end,
discernable motion or bend,
as the steaming sleep of history: neither given or giver.
It needs a dull moon
to define its surface, that membrane between shiver and
   still
the thickness of bestial will;
it needs the fish to divine its currents; it needs the stone
to confine its depths.
Definition explained by form. Is that all I am to be? Can
   be?
A shadow from the sea?

I wish to be more or less than moon; more or less than
    fish; more
or less than brother to the stone.

III

Her blood is blind, predictable to the point
of tedium, yet runs the dark with righteous intensity.
Such mindlessness needs no reason,
needs no acquaintance with the seasons
of the heart to firm its resolve. It is, and to be less is not
    to be.

Her blood is blind, unaware of its biographies:
the rushing fragments of her father, himself a brutal son;
the bright flake of mortal pain
hacked from a caveless plain;
pieces of the world before worlds, world before One.

Her blood is blind, and she sleeps.
I am made to see, and do not. Which of us is more cruelly
    disowned?
For a thousand nights we've slept.
For thousands more she will sleep,
weaving the deep, safe from haunting, as I arise, and drown.

kenilworth

it stands firm
upon its hill
            incomplete.
sky glazes
the great arched windows.
stepworn stairs
fall short of rooms.
the gates are frozen shut.
its ragged walls belong
to doves, and trailing vines.

upon its hill,
it stands firm,
            solitary,
seeming to need no more
than birds and vines
to shoulder the seasons
once again turning,
surviving the shadows best
when before its autistic stare
            the night
            comes to kneel

                    *   *

In our time,
we rode the bridge over that ragged rill,
ascended the winter hill
and saw her rise from the snow,

15

red as a stormbroken sun, saw this misted
                    by the plumes of our breath.
She rocked in our sight as we approached.
She meant the loosed weight of our weapons,
wine, friends,
fires to draw the warm stink from our furs,
and sleep
while the sharp stars plunged

                    in our time.

                    *   *

We clashed in the tilting yard to celebrate the seasons,
as pennants cracked in the wind.
The grass was never so green as on those afternoons,
never as rich without the thunder of the gallop,
                    and flashes of silver.

The trumpets soared,
and seemed to pull the sound from our throats

and we, the combatants,
sat heavily on nervous horses,
hearts and breath booming in our helmets,
staring,
waiting over our slit of ground,
locked in that same visible moment
                    before the juggler's ball
                    descends.

                    *   *

16

We lords proposed and eluded treachery,
and carefully judged our allegiances
among the staggering shadows
                        of lantern flame.

We soldiers auctioned off our loyalty,
and repaid it at the streams
in horrible arcs,
often sagging in our saddles as our limbs
                        splashed,
                        and settled under.

And we, the others,
our fingers numb to the touch of all
but naked skin,
wondered who would be next,
who would then claim or kill us,
                        and endured.

                *   *

We sat noisily around heaped tables
until we reeled and vomited,
our lungs and eyes burning with firesmoke,
a pageant of leiges and ladies,
lovers, soldiers and sons.
We could see without knowing
the transience of this holy place.
We could hear without remembering
the hollowness of our fealty.

And we could laugh without crying
at the truth of the jesters, insane with colors,
who came and went with the music,

                    dancing in,
                    dancing on

Terra Nova (1912):
Kathleen Scott Sails to Meet the Captain

The world changes.
England is changing, Kathleen.
Lanes that led to love
have begun to run backwards.
The billowing, stonewalled meadows
are falling to bleakness and rubble.
The maternal whispers of summer leaves
are becoming somber as the chants of monks.
                    And the birds
                    are learning the psalms.

The world changes.
Kathleen, the sea is changing
beneath you, as you slide Southward
in its broad, strong palm.
It is becoming grey and mean,
and will claw at the black home rock,
a thief of seasons, an ogre god
whose spell gives the men who sail it
                    youth
                    and his smile.

We change.
You are changing, Kathleen.
The girls and women you were
are hurrying ahead to meet you.
The blaze of coming mornings
is arcing behind you.

At the dock, a man who cannot look up
will hand you vastness and struggle.
                    And your eyes will seek out
                    the children who are lonely.

We change.
Kathleen, you are changing
into an apparition, a dream.
And he, as dream, is coming to life.
Far away, in the manger of the wind,
your heart drums in a slush of sleep and waking,
in a vague stench of fouled breath,
heat's last feeble promise,
                    as days glide like mimes
                    from the lantern.

Everything changes.
Times are changing, Kathleen.
You will see that he covered his ears and grieved
when they killed the ponies for meat,
and understand
as well as you understand your journey.
He will not have decided this end;
but isn't the choosing of honor, in itself, the same?
                    As futures glide like mimes
                    from your cabin lamp.

Eyes to ice.
Bone to stone.
Pliant flesh becomes the mountain face.
The change is made in guttering

lantern afternoon light on English lawns,
at tables in cool grottoes of shade
where they toast his achievement, and he smiles
and lifts his wine to you, and the afternoon light,
                              deep, warm light,
                              such grand light
                              for ponies and men . . . .

21

western hero

The product of a scorpion and a snake
                              you say.
Pillar of stone. Glitter rimmed with dust.
Slit-mouthed. And for all this you love me.

My right hand with its boyhood broken finger
                              would sooner
smile over the curves of a gun butt
than hold a heavy breast. Yet you love me.

You are paying now for the charged men
                              I lifted
and set down in a tangle of torn meat,
a starred splash, paying for love of me.

My lives were not numbered or noble
                              or needed.
Merely adaptations to powers nonexistent,
and missed in blue light. I never loved you.
So leave me be.
Let me die.

marion, ohio

noon's golden boats
heeled on the parking lot

ladies in broad hats
affected tennis on my lawn

servants murmured
in the halls of the church

        it stays on, bewildered
        as its memories blink out
        one by one —
        sirens in deep morning

and handsome warren waltzed
the gray and dying girls . . . .

petroglyphs
(hawaii)

ships with bellied sails, fish, turtles, skied birds,
                                        hunters,
lie scattered in the meadow, gray, where the ocean
once was. A stick-figure man and woman
hold the hands of a child between them. a portrait.
                              See how we lived.

we part the high grass and kneel to the stone;
                                        unfurl
our linen squares and trace the rough grooves
with colors. A green crab rises. A blue fish.
2,000 years from the sea. there is nothing to say.
                              See what we were.

weak light, yellow on the trees. we go quietly,
                                        leave
the rocks sinking into the ground, going under,
going back, space empty of ripple and sound,
fish, turtles, birds, ships with bellied sails.
                              We lived!

substratum

enter the fat earth.
rappel carefully down
the striped well-side . . .
see how it all came about,
youth to age, strong to weak,
the loss of essential malice.
touch it, feel it
in your dark veins,
the once-warm world
full and open to sun,
now folded in stone, faded
as remembered flowers.

study the prints
of layered love,
each creating another
of more intricate design . . .
see how the tender skin
hardened into armor,
how the stammering touch
became cool and poised,
how from each innocence
evolved a higher form of doubt . . .
eternal thyme
of rock upon rock.

press against it .
recall grass, sky,
beasts and birds,
mountainous clouds . . .
the endless seams
of loss and gain.
hold the young bone,
time's champion
before you, now,
bone-hunter
life-hunter
of morning mirrors.

IN THE HORSE LATITUDES

latitude 12º 46' N.,
longitude 25º 05' W.

a long time
we've lain still
waiting for wind.
we mark emptiness
to the horizons.
day upon day
we remember where
we should be now.
it gets inside
and we work hard
at nothing, work
the same jobs
over and over
to keep from killing
one another,
and become obsessed
with knives.
at sudden nightfall
we pray:
perhaps tomorrow.
and wait
and wait
and wait

Hotel Rio

years ago, or maybe yesterday,
Biederman stopped his curbward lurch
and stood fumbling in loose-gutted misery
and glanced up, by chance, at a second-story window
and saw breasts —
> beautiful, heavy, globed, perfect breasts
> that stilled him to stone
> young breasts (he remembered their look)
radiant above the violet fumes of a sign:
> HOTEL RIO
and he stared until he sobbed
and crumbled down piecemeal
> knowing what he wanted, then.

they tried to kill him, Biederman,
the old bastard, when someone found out
he was hoarding money, but he beat away
their scabbed, mucous-slick faces with a bottle-neck
and a trash can lid —
> sending them, his friends, falling
> and crying and jumping furiously
> back into their icy corners
and he hurried his shuffling steps
> down streets
known only by their lights, his soul
wrapped around a celery bag in his coat:
> enough money to die in scotch.

two guys threw him out, old Biederman,
when he went into the men's room
at the gas station. but he managed
to wash and shave before they broke in
and kicked him along.
                    he wandered for hours in the cold
                    holding himself together, trying hard
                    to remember where the violet sign was
and what the name was, and saw:
                    THE MUSTANG HOTEL
and he laughed out loud
and stuttered across the road
                    knowing where he was at last.

everybody had a good laugh on him,
fruitcake Biederman, when he opened up
his celery bag and bought a night.
he laughed, too, a little, and stared
at his broken shoes.
                    take your pick, old fella.
                    but how could he tell? the breasts . . .
                    he couldn't tell, from the steel-bound
                        faces,
which one she was, so he said:
                    please
take off the tops, I'm looking for
someone I saw one time — and they got mad
                    and screamed all around him.

31

he was rushed and confused, Biederman,
but it was okay. he'd found her, he was sure,
at the last minute, and they went upstairs,
and she stripped. they were just like he remembered,
    young,
heavy, perfect,

                    and he lay down with her
                    and pressed his face against them.
                    I just want to sleep here, like this, he
                        said,
that's all. and after awhile he woke up
                    and looked
past the curve of her neck, looked out through
the window where it was snowing in the night,
                    cold and clean and pure.

ruins

the car mountains —
old and changing. I see that.
I know.

but look at the characters.
one with his mouth open,
blind eyes turned up.
one mangled but still fighting,
with teeth showing and fingerless fists low.
one just dozing off.
and they're quiet about it.

jefferson davis was my cat.
he was a good ratter.
he must of headed south
when the tupelo burned.
it don't really matter why.

the fence needs fixing.
but I like the looks of it.

inside I got a list.
it says on it —
        california
        new york
        miami
        mexico
        the ocean
I've had it since I was twenty.

33

spring.
rain runs off their lips.
rust crawls. metal thins.

the year's back.

washington square

Sunday noon —
electric fantasies flare and fade on the landscape
and from the sun and smells of unity
a raggedy-coated black man came at me
with his hands out, grinning,
one eye blind and white,
saying, 'Uncle, Uncle, where you been?'
He followed me for half an hour, *me*,
white boy,
crying, 'Uncle, Uncle, wait for me'
and I did not call him my own,
for which I will surely
                be damned.

pisces

she waved her hand and ran to catch up,
moving at once through numb space
and into an evening's quietus,
the fluid center of an ache, subtle as the pain of imagined
    burns.

this was her imparted second, her alter life,
in which she will be loved beyond bounds
or contrivance, without even realizing it.
she will have her phantom comforts, and strains of
    impossible weight

but once always she ran to catch up,
glorious, and once always there were no surprises,
only wonders
good and bad.

early violets

Cells of memory blossom
like early violets
from a spring of raw timber
and an attitude of boots.
How long has it been? Ten years?
More, since I've had nothing to do
                              but love you.

These are days of dull warmth,
and abstractions now easier to chase
because of their distance: spirit,
truth, beauty, space — all
connected to this larger source
more difficult to trace, yet easiest
                              to pronounce.

It's best to let it be, I suppose.
Best not to analyze, but summarize
in the generalities of seasons, moons,
and the moments of them. Best just to say
that it's you who yearns for the sea,
but me who dreams of sailing ships
                              running before the wind.

the adventurer

a maverick shadow, shuffling
    in mute discontent,
plucked her from a tantrum of rain,
    coveted her in haze
for a brief moment, then gave her up —
    and I saw her
come nearer, as if moving through an open room
    in moon's light,
sleek and finely drawn, her naked face
    unaware
and betrayed by subliminal promises
    of breathlessness.

When I turned, she had run behind
    some edge
and I continued on in the city's slash,
    shaken and afraid
of implications, but eagerly invoking
    guiltless eyes
and the warm slip of her tongue on my lips,
    and the path
of a voyaging hand alive, alive, alive
    with rose's flame.

stepson

the ritual runs to bravery tales
and unsupportable knowledge.
                               you can hear the strut.

lines are drawn and crossed.
warnings are rehearsed
                               on jury-rigged sets.

gouged flesh is painless,
worth no more than
                               a rueful smile.

someday, when it's done,
we'll have a beer.
                               it'll be all right.

we pass in the hallway
                               like new recruits.

the summer after he died

the words glittered
like flying bits of metal
as she talked about her children,
neighbors, grass paling with heat,
how busy she was now.
                        her bloodless hands,
skeletal with wishes,
fluttered in the light,
lifting and lowering a hammer,
pinching tacks, re-covering
                        his chair.

the seventies

when he worked late
he stayed until dawn,
because his office was secure.
outside and inside the doors were locked.
there was brightness all around him,
and long halls.

out there, others curled against the cold
like spoons.
but he was safe.

and he would never leave
without first light at his shoulder,
afraid to nausea
of running the razored parking lot
and reaching his car
unassaulted.

commuter

Darkness stays longer now.
Rootless shoes call up the cold.
Breath billows, as from the nostrils of oxen.
We jockey for places on the 5:15.

Smoke, coats, paper, whiskey, damp hair.
Gray smells that rise and return.
A dull ghost's face against the glass
dreading discovery of the missing among us.

I'm still here. Hair soaked with snow.
Four lanes away, a wife and sons
move in lighted stalls, waiting for me.
I watch from the dark, unmoving, afraid for my
    life.

the monster

her phone rang
with a distant machine gun's rattle,
putting me in mind of a valley
and armed camps in the snow . . .
a place I've never been, but often feel.
                    hello?
I didn't answer quickly.
purpose wandered.
headless words arose like futures,
but nothing I could hold or look down the line of
and I did not answer.
                    hello?
everything fled but dark alertness.
I heard fear, fear, of all things,
of me, whom her lifted hips have kissed
countless times.
but it was not me. it was unseen,
uncommitted, no more than a breathing.
the thought was awesome in its fright.
not me yet, would not be until I spoke,
and still I did not speak,
but saw her infinitely then,
drew her from past terrors and saw
the razor of white between her lips
and her mottling cheeks,
and crossed over an irreversible border.
I stood
and watched her see some cold raider try the door
and the room implode,

watched her see her own deep flesh hammered and
    slashed,
her own blood blowing loose . . .
                    who is this?
her voice sailed and beat
and saved me.
I burst open, racing my excuses to jam the door,
bad connection thought it was a wrong number was
    distracted,
fueled by the rolling sweat under my shirt
and my bellowing heart.

it's been years since.
she doesn't remember dying anymore.
but I haven't forgotten,
and haven't told her that I saw it clearly
for a moment,
felt it,
older than any mud-built god,
that horrible   love.

evidence

We did not see the wind . . .
only evidence of its passing
in the leaves, the grass, the clothes
on the line.

We did not hear the wind . . .
only evidence of its passing
in the distant sigh of a train,
in far bell song.

Then your hand touched mine
with its visions of night fears,
pretended rage, food tearing.
Evidence, too.

glimpses

waiting blue within the wind is crying,
and denying shapes of touch
which flash and fly silvered from underhand
to grand clear light. but such
lights are as sourceless as rushing streams
or dreaming pose of history.
the ends of endless threads spun by mystery
from sight and shade —
in the brightness of my night
in the darkness of your days.

breached panic, last jagged, folded to flower
and towering castle cloud,
the boldest notes in a country of the mind —
I find he always talks aloud
and travels afoot down empty winding lanes
in gentle rain. and I make the sun
unmoving and mild, to burn on only one
whom sight has made
in the brightness of my night
in the darkness of your days.

waiting blue within, swarming storm without,
and about the solid lovers
brush and glide. but the faceless voice
has no choice of cover;
it is as true as close trembling, or the drying cheek
that seeks my own
from a tangential blindness, mirror shown.

it is polite to stay
in the brightness of my night
in the darkness of your days.

verges

We pace on verges willingly met.
Affix pain to days that will come again.
Settle with a dream of distance.
                    We wonder.

Inventors of time, the club,
                    forgiveness.

This love of endings   and unimagined arrivals
                    a fear
                    in the blood.

the real world

he awoke
in the ache and heat of boot camp,
opened his eyes to living
on false walls and high nets,
in the bump and growl of his helmet.
his rifle was made for his hands.

he grew up at normandy
in the shade of glider wings and sound,
then fell into poses,
dented helmet cocked and rifle stock on his hip,
for the kids
puking quietly between their boots.
he was larger than myself
a hero, a god
to be loved forever.

he left a leg in belgium
and died when I touched new york.
he was all I could ever have been.
and sometimes, at meetings over lunch, he comes
deep-eyed
fierce in the roaring dust,
touching the talk around me to wordless babble,
calling me back from the grave.

animal

Animal went six-seven and two-sixty.
made his Harley look like a Big Wheel.
he liked to say he was the country's leading philanthropist
    of fear:
               no matter how little he had himself,
               he always gave twice as much to others.

he loved words like squash and pound
and stomp and smash . . . words that phonetically
contained both the moment of violence and its aftermath.
               but he also liked the sounds of impact:
               hit, crack, smack, belt.

he laughed a lot; he was happy as hell.
he got a real charge out of hurting people,
like crushing their hands in his own, then working the
    bones around.
               a lot of guys say they're going to kill
                 him.
               but he seems a million years old already.

jackson miss

straight from the cottonmouth:
"dinnertime" is noon dahn heah.
ya'll in the Sath now,
     (asshole)

    **

great green centipedes waver up
and swallow the anchor cables of telephone poles —
stare down miles of hot meat
      towards jackson.
you know, fellas, I've told this story a hundred times
and no one's ever believed me, but in 1945 when I was
stationed in Marienbad . . .

    **

whipped niggers, quiet, floating
     in the fields . . . .

    **

now *she's* beautiful, honey-mouthed,
talking with her eyes and hands too about fried snapper
 throats
and loving us all with carnage.

    **

bill says of grits: *well, it looks like Cream a Wheat,*
but it's really cream a corn tops, and tastes like cream
 a shit.

**

there's this restaurant:
Carlie weighs in at about three hundred
puts her bare feet up on the table
and stares at you and rocks in her chair
and you eat whatever her girls put in front of you
                              all of it
or she'll call you names and charge you double.
who could love such an obscenity?
                              who couldn't?

I been here two years now, the salesman trembles.
and I don't miss it up North. no sir. I like it here.
but I could leave in a minute
and never look back.
while he pours himself three fingers' worth
and stretches out his legs and sips,
thoughtfully watching the snakes
                              in his swimming pool.

sliproot canyon

The wind, she's got teeth tonight. Might be
she got her bitter bite from the last clean ice
no boot has scored. Funneled it through
some northern border town still waiting
for the experience of heat. I can't ask for less.

She hammers the rock. Sends bubbles of buckshot
and choking cold breaking over these two warm lives.
North Slope oil. Lakes rotten to fifty foot down.
Issues. The facts are here in the howl and bash,
ice stiff mane, my frozen hands.

It ain't mine
to spoil or save.

fire shows

I

in subaqueous light, one dying planet flares
and sears the musky universe.
other planets go to spitting flame,
so on and on the road of suns.
light grows to its limits
                    hovers
                        and cracks.

ancient fire shows.
one leaf ignites,
a widowed word.

it flickers in the wind.

II

nothing's changed still.
getting back into it's as easy as falling in a hole.
morning serpents swinging box heads
one eye black and one red
greasy thumb prints on the OFF from the graveyard trick,
                         and the station stinks.
they never stop,
the inviolate voices of iron,
just like yesterday or next year,
whoop groan chatter bang whine
ratcheting overhead, over the mountains and edges,
under the firmament of light without shadow —
bloodless unhooded idiot stare, hourless as death,
                         colder than hate.
creation's cave.
the air smells of burn.

*   *   *

set hook pick move drop retrieve set hook pick
move drop retrieve set hook pick move drop retrieve set hook pick move drop retrieve set
hey, man hook *you do that real well* pick *you
been practicin'?* move *up your ass* drop *how 'bout
a beer after?* retrieve *that sounds good* set hook
pick move drop retrieve set hook pick move drop
retrieve set hook move . . . *hey, shit, Jesus Christ
you trynna kill me, asshole? huh? sorry, already . . .*
pick move drop retrieve set hook pick move drop
retrieve set hook pick move drop retrieve set
hook pick move drop retrieve set hook . . . *what's
goin' on here? what happened? I made a little
mistake, I missed my beat is all. no big deal,
already. oh, yeah? mistakes get people killed,
dummy. mistakes get people canned from their job.
you never made a mistake, huh? you run this
lousy bitch hoist all day and try . . . you don't
like it, take off, why don't you. I'm talkin' to
the steward about you, man, I'm . . . you're doin'
shit. I'm gonna do you a big favor and pass on the
write-up 'cause you been here so long, but you
do anything like that again, and . . . I ain't gonna
do it again. I just missed my beat, that's all.
okay, then. move it. you're holdin' up the line.*
pick move drop retrieve set hook pick move drop
retrieve set hook pick move drop retrieve set hook
pick move drop retrieve set hook pick move drop
retrieve set hook pick move drop retrieve set
hook pick move drop retrieve set hook pick move
drop retrieve *I'm gonna bust his face someday*

56

set hook pick move drop retrieve set hook pick
move drop retrieve set hook pick move drop
retrieve set hook pick move drop retrieve *I'm*
gonna get the hell out of here someday set hook
pick move drop retrieve set hook pick move drop
retrieve set hook pick move drop retrieve set hook
pick move drop retrieve set hook pick move drop
retrieve set hook pick move drop retrieve set hook
pick move drop retrieve *I am* . . .

* * *

the klaxon echoes.
bologna and mayonnaise and cookies and an apple
and a thermos of coffee and vodka, half empty
already. *God, I hate bologna.*

*hey, Kelly says he's gonna stick your head in
the shaper to get rid of that ugly wart on your
face. but I tole him you need it 'cause you breathe
through it.*

laughter.
Colosante's a funny guy.

*   *   *

set hook pick move drop retrieve set hook pick
move drop retrieve set hook pick move drop retrieve set hook pick move drop retrieve set hook
pick move drop retrieve set hook pick move drop
retrieve *what time is it?* set hook pick move
drop retrieve set hook pick move drop retrieve
set hook pick move drop retrieve set hook pick
move drop retrieve set hook pick move drop retrieve set hook pick move drop retrieve set hook
pick move drop retrieve *what time is it?* set
hook pick move drop retrieve set hook pick move
drop retrieve set hook pick move drop retrieve
set hook pick move drop retrieve set hook pick
move drop retrieve set hook pick move drop retrieve set hook pick move drop retrieve set hook
pick move drop retrieve set hook pick move drop
retrieve set hook pick move drop retrieve set hook
pick move drop retrieve *what time is it?*

III

there is a glow in the wine,
at its center there,
the furnaces, like vaults in the sea.
the smokestacks shimmer apart
and rebuild beyond counting,
until the tremble, scar and patches of dead skin
are covered,
cooled enough
        to create a night's love.

day's end.
shy armies of cripples
crawl to fires in the dust.

seascape

(ex nihilo, ad nihilo)

I

Baile Atha Cliath.
Masted words, true to themselves.
Shapes of ships tilting, sweeping to edge and point
from black seas under . . . a dark nearness,
spatial displacement that crowds the dream into eloquence
without soul or intent . . .
and along the shore latched wood butts the night
patient for the morning's windy wheel and shriek,
the knock of a pipe bowl against a wall,
clattering steps

        on the cobblestones.

II

A fog on the brain as he walks blunt-eyed along
    Fisherman's Wharf
in peacoat and watch cap, fogged in,
the Invisible Man marching past the magic shops
and Ripley's House of genetic blanks,
being jostled by tourists wondering where the freaks go
    for fun
and also in a hurry to hit Ghiradelli Square
before descending the hill to kaleidoscopic orgasms in
    North Beach
at the fluted end of Chinatown
                 ("never seen so many foreigners
                      in one place in mah life.")

Aware of placelessness — let's see now
above are muslin hills to Sacramento,
and below the King's Highway with its abstractions
of ocean/beach/rock seen from atop draped cliffs,
Airstream trailers parked in flatland camps
and the smoky remotes of L.A. and on to the ovens of
    Mexico,
then, beside, landsward, the great grassy breast of
    America
with its oddly lined overlay of Indian names in Helvetica
    Bold,
as vast and whole in its people's hearts as Russia,
                   a cold day's journey away . . .

III

From a sea, of sorts,
given to pressures, tidal disturbances,
cosmic rumblings on occasion.
A humorless shipping out.
Sound drums the water.
Molecules knit webs of matter into constructions
of invented time.
The deeps drifter is lashed amidships with spiralling cable,
daily growing more eager for land and light,
tired of transience by now,
of star charting and tasteless food,
and the creaking of constellations on the lips of waves.
Breathless in a sea of sorts.
Unremembered infinity.

how do little fella aw look at him he's a moose alright
      look
at the hands on that kid the next heavyweight champ he
      looks
just like his dad oh thank you its lovely thought he might
      need
it he may be too young for it now but it should fit in a
      few
have a drink on that yes thanks don't mind if I do join me
of course hi there hi can you smile gimme a big smile ah
ha ha that's a boy oh I remember when our little ones

'gah', says he
and dribbles a yo-yo studded with crumbs.

ha ha look at the little bugger oh my let me clean you up
ha ha say did you catch that thanks well cheers congratu-
      lations
thank you thank you thank you

Toys that click.
Sunlight
on the playroom floor.

IV

What's left now
in the progression from the sea —
reflections from an anchor-stamped peacoat button.
Sweetheart, boy, son, name
honey, dad, mister, name
grandpa, dear departed —
all behind and ahead,
he's deep in the shit now,
in the hot breath of a future like no other,
fearful and needing a sign.
It's more than age.
Who will take care of me when I am old?
How can I live?
And he stands alone on the beach
in dull dawn light stirred by gulls,
waves hissing in,
watches a jogger slowly rise gray from the sand,
come a long way,
pass in measured rhythms and shrink away again,
a ghost come and gone
leaving greater loneliness
than he takes.

Early runner.
Like that.
Like that.

from Matthew

Grandfather, look at me.
At my eyes.
Tell me what I remember.
From your gray stone and smoke
and silent walks with the Christmas fire,
talk of heather that flows like evening sky
down the flanks of bonnie bens;
of the thunder of shrouded torrents, of glens,
and the somber lochs where mountains swim.
Build me a high castle and tumble it down again
                    to make a byre for the cows.
                    Teach me to taste the names.

Grandfather, talk to me
of struggle.
Tell me how the clans descended.
Talk of how the wretched armies came down
from the wilderness, from the black houses stumbled
with pikes and stones and minds aglow with uncertainty
to the sad Culloden plain; how they fought and died.
Show me the crimson English sea that waits ashamed
as the ruined boys come again, again, through the
    cannon's fog
stepping to the drum, unfurling the piper's song.
                    Tell me the legends of mist,
                    so I'll know to be strong.

Grandfather, sing to me
in prancing rhyme

Lover's pledges beside the tarns;
of granite horsemen riding in anger,
and men in boots who hunt the rolling shoals of haddie.
Sing me the straths of morning.
And the father to the son who sleeps at his breast,
he no bigger than a young lad's dream:
— You've also a heart beats twice, my boy.
And it's once for God, and once for the highland green. —
                              Sing to the child.
                              The man will hear.

the sin-eaters

long shapes hover beside the creek, seeing
the shimmer of bitter fires on the water —

they shovel flaming ground, hearing whispered tales
of mangled limbs and morning wars —

they cup cold, weed-lipped railroad tracks, feeling
the shiver and blast of greasy cannons —

they breathe sweet wind on stone-marked hills, smelling
the corpses of sunburned soldiers and bloated horses —

they tongue names: Gettysburg, Chattanooga, Atlanta,
    tasting
bloody leaves and the sly horror of sharp smoke —

mouth smiles accuse; stony eyes buried in brim-shade
are gorged, gorged, and hungering for more.

house

Footworn stone, upwound —
a touch of dry moss.
    The air thrums:
eulogies, and forgotten madrigals.
And a contrapuntal bell,
    open-mouthed, blind sound,
pressing cities in pages of orange light.
My house of gathered hearts,
all as silent and untrusting
    as birds.

*   *

My house: easy-breathing seas and swallowed sails,
a ridden swell.
    Every upright soul is a victim.
And the canvas fields, frail with stars.
They keen and wheel,
    the birds,
sowing chains of gray bubbles.
My house of aggregate space,
    crowding the ruins.

*   *

Jagged canyons beat in the cold and driven shadow.
    Boots drum.
And the energy is laughter in lighter flash,
    in the faces of fishy boys
up from the boats.

I hide alone, chilled.
Dawn rises around us
    like a life.

*   *

My house.   Doors
            without rooms.

still life

(to an overheard wish that one could paint
a picture a day on a single canvas, so he
could leave behind images of his life, layer
upon layer, as they happened.)

The canvas, stretched and struggling under rocket-sewn
    skies,
a last wavering line in blue (it must be blue),
is all that remains.

Begun with a wavering stroke, ended with the same,
but clouded with the days between, the last not so clear
    as the first,
is all there ever was.

And peeling back to beginnings we cross your ages,
your dreams and copulations, to the first brush stroke —
then nothing.

Do you really think the memory would be of that first
    color?
No. It would be of the whole, the blur of your small
    crawlings
on hands and knees, your dying in the suns of a thousand
imagined afternoons.

71

It Doesn't Rhyme, He Said
(for J.R.)

a poem is a shape,
        a fossil,
           the crystal of a radio.
it is the tiny bones
        of light.

*   *   *

history rhymes.
as the world tumbles on, its times
re-appear, our bonds to the moon and seas
will never change. nor the religions of a breeze.
nor our relief as the red sun climbs.
history rhymes.

*   *   *

love rhymes.
the clarity of grace entwines
numberless filaments of thought. it is not for the
    bold,
but the fearful. it is what holds
them to the earth. as the wind is to chimes.
love rhymes.

*   *   *

sudden death
and abrupt swervings of the future
                    call for consonants,
            and words that crack
                        or shatter.
death is orange
and will not rhyme.

*　　*　　*

from a dented sky, gray and low,
the first dry seed of winter comes wandering
over the fences and grizzled fields,
searching for a place to land, and grow.
                    the cows look up
                    for the man who brings them hay.
and in the bare bones of a tree,
the flicker of a cardinal's wing,
a single light left burning   at the doorway   to Spring.

*　　*　　*

a rhyme is not made;
it presents itself.

home again

The doctor said
he was ready to go back,
but it would be more difficult for them.
He must remember
that at the end of all the years
is the morning they combed his hair
                         for the last time.

He chose summer
for returning. Their welcome
was broken and mended many times
by the assumptions of his face.
The confrontation ended
when her fingers lightly smoothed his tie
                         and drew away.

He remembers,
and feels their hardened days,
standing in the doorway to his room
where even the sunlight
had not been moved.
His turn now to awaken

                    the vanished child.

them

Eventually they will come,
scattered amber flung landward from the gulf.
We will have feared patiently.

We've always known they will come
to end our history, justify our will, to whisper down
all our gods but one.

Perhaps they will come soon,
skimming the seas and fields, angels arrived,
at last giving us ourselves.

MAYBE WE'LL LIVE

harbinger

The border walker
stalks across my window world,
rain-boned, cloud crowded,
with his boots and jeans and giant strides,
jacket full of wind —
and on the morning side of drizzling fence
the earth humps up like a boxer
struggling to his knees.

Mud boy,
mean life muscling up and out
through winter's furtive ice —
the spirit always comprehends first, and stirs
from its deep sleep curl
as he marches past, chin high, hair flying,
shouting voiceless down
the mirror floated road.

it's no matter
for inquiry by historians,
or concern, or even thought
in the taut slip of days,
the seasons going their ways,
turning —

it's no cause
for an interrupted step,
or sudden recollection,
or question, or deep gaze
eased from a quiet and gray
morning.

But I was here
      once.